From (date) _____

To (date) _____

O W N E R

_____

_____

_____

_____

Address

_____

Phone

_____

Email Address

NOTES

Credit Card Information

Credit Card Info	Name on Card	Number	Exp. Date	Code

Banking (Checking/Savings) Information

Account Type (Checking/Savings)	Name on Account	Account Number	Routing Number

Online Account Information

Company	ID/Login	Password	Notes

Security ? #1	Security ? #2	Security ? #3	Security ? #4
Security Answer #1	Security Answer #2	Security Answer #3	Security Answer #4

Company	ID/Login	Password	Notes

Security ? #1	Security ? #2	Security ? #3	Security ? #4
Security Answer #1	Security Answer #2	Security Answer #3	Security Answer #4

Company	ID/Login	Password	Notes

Security ? #1	Security ? #2	Security ? #3	Security ? #4
Security Answer #1	Security Answer #2	Security Answer #3	Security Answer #4

Company	ID/Login	Password	Notes

Security ? #1	Security ? #2	Security ? #3	Security ? #4
Security Answer #1	Security Answer #2	Security Answer #3	Security Answer #4

Company	ID/Login	Password	Notes

Security ? #1	Security ? #2	Security ? #3	Security ? #4
Security Answer #1	Security Answer #2	Security Answer #3	Security Answer #4

Company	ID/Login	Password	Notes

Security ? #1	Security ? #2	Security ? #3	Security ? #4
Security Answer #1	Security Answer #2	Security Answer #3	Security Answer #4

Company	ID/Login	Password	Notes

Security ? #1	Security ? #2	Security ? #3	Security ? #4
Security Answer #1	Security Answer #2	Security Answer #3	Security Answer #4

Online Account Information

Company	ID/Login	Password	Notes

Security ? #1	Security ? #2	Security ? #3	Security ? #4
Security Answer #1	Security Answer #2	Security Answer #3	Security Answer #4

Company	ID/Login	Password	Notes

Security ? #1	Security ? #2	Security ? #3	Security ? #4
Security Answer #1	Security Answer #2	Security Answer #3	Security Answer #4

Company	ID/Login	Password	Notes

Security ? #1	Security ? #2	Security ? #3	Security ? #4
Security Answer #1	Security Answer #2	Security Answer #3	Security Answer #4

Company	ID/Login	Password	Notes

Security ? #1	Security ? #2	Security ? #3	Security ? #4
Security Answer #1	Security Answer #2	Security Answer #3	Security Answer #4

Company	ID/Login	Password	Notes

Security ? #1	Security ? #2	Security ? #3	Security ? #4
Security Answer #1	Security Answer #2	Security Answer #3	Security Answer #4

Company	ID/Login	Password	Notes

Security ? #1	Security ? #2	Security ? #3	Security ? #4
Security Answer #1	Security Answer #2	Security Answer #3	Security Answer #4

Company	ID/Login	Password	Notes

Security ? #1	Security ? #2	Security ? #3	Security ? #4
Security Answer #1	Security Answer #2	Security Answer #3	Security Answer #4

Online Account Information

Company	ID/Login	Password	Notes

Security ? #1	Security ? #2	Security ? #3	Security ? #4
Security Answer #1	Security Answer #2	Security Answer #3	Security Answer #4

Company	ID/Login	Password	Notes

Security ? #1	Security ? #2	Security ? #3	Security ? #4
Security Answer #1	Security Answer #2	Security Answer #3	Security Answer #4

Company	ID/Login	Password	Notes

Security ? #1	Security ? #2	Security ? #3	Security ? #4
Security Answer #1	Security Answer #2	Security Answer #3	Security Answer #4

Company	ID/Login	Password	Notes

Security ? #1	Security ? #2	Security ? #3	Security ? #4
Security Answer #1	Security Answer #2	Security Answer #3	Security Answer #4

Company	ID/Login	Password	Notes

Security ? #1	Security ? #2	Security ? #3	Security ? #4
Security Answer #1	Security Answer #2	Security Answer #3	Security Answer #4

Company	ID/Login	Password	Notes

Security ? #1	Security ? #2	Security ? #3	Security ? #4
Security Answer #1	Security Answer #2	Security Answer #3	Security Answer #4

Company	ID/Login	Password	Notes

Security ? #1	Security ? #2	Security ? #3	Security ? #4
Security Answer #1	Security Answer #2	Security Answer #3	Security Answer #4

Online Account Information

Company	ID/Login	Password	Notes	

Security ? #1	Security ? #2	Security ? #3	Security ? #4
Security Answer #1	Security Answer #2	Security Answer #3	Security Answer #4

Company	ID/Login	Password	Notes	

Security ? #1	Security ? #2	Security ? #3	Security ? #4
Security Answer #1	Security Answer #2	Security Answer #3	Security Answer #4

Company	ID/Login	Password	Notes	

Security ? #1	Security ? #2	Security ? #3	Security ? #4
Security Answer #1	Security Answer #2	Security Answer #3	Security Answer #4

Company	ID/Login	Password	Notes	

Security ? #1	Security ? #2	Security ? #3	Security ? #4
Security Answer #1	Security Answer #2	Security Answer #3	Security Answer #4

Company	ID/Login	Password	Notes	

Security ? #1	Security ? #2	Security ? #3	Security ? #4
Security Answer #1	Security Answer #2	Security Answer #3	Security Answer #4

Company	ID/Login	Password	Notes	

Security ? #1	Security ? #2	Security ? #3	Security ? #4
Security Answer #1	Security Answer #2	Security Answer #3	Security Answer #4

Company	ID/Login	Password	Notes	

Security ? #1	Security ? #2	Security ? #3	Security ? #4
Security Answer #1	Security Answer #2	Security Answer #3	Security Answer #4

JANUARY _____

Due Date	Bill Description	Amount Due	Amount Paid	Paid Date	Confirmation Number	Notes

Notes for the Month

_____

_____

_____

_____

_____

_____

_____

_____

_____

_____

_____

NOTES

February _____

Due Date	Bill Description	Amount Due	Amount Paid	Paid Date	Confirmation Number	Notes

Notes for the Month

_____
_____
_____
_____
_____
_____
_____
_____
_____
_____
_____

NOTES

March _____

Due Date	Bill Description	Amount Due	Amount Paid	Paid Date	Confirmation Number	Notes

Notes for the Month

_____
_____
_____
_____
_____
_____
_____
_____
_____
_____

April _____

Due Date	Bill Description	Amount Due	Amount Paid	Paid Date	Confirmation Number	Notes

Notes for the Month

_____
_____
_____
_____
_____
_____
_____
_____
_____
_____
_____
_____

NOTES

May _____

Due Date	Bill Description	Amount Due	Amount Paid	Paid Date	Confirmation Number	Notes

Notes for the Month

_____
_____
_____
_____
_____
_____
_____
_____
_____
_____
_____

NOTES

June _____

Due Date	Bill Description	Amount Due	Amount Paid	Paid Date	Confirmation Number	Notes

Notes for the Month

_____
_____
_____
_____
_____
_____
_____
_____
_____
_____
_____

NOTES

July _____

Due Date	Bill Description	Amount Due	Amount Paid	Paid Date	Confirmation Number	Notes

Notes for the Month

NOTES

NOTES

August _____

Due Date	Bill Description	Amount Due	Amount Paid	Paid Date	Confirmation Number	Notes

Notes for the Month

_____

_____

_____

_____

_____

_____

_____

_____

_____

_____

_____

NOTES

September _____

Due Date	Bill Description	Amount Due	Amount Paid	Paid Date	Confirmation Number	Notes

Notes for the Month

_____
_____
_____
_____
_____
_____
_____
_____
_____
_____

NOTES

October _____

Due Date	Bill Description	Amount Due	Amount Paid	Paid Date	Confirmation Number	Notes

Notes for the Month

_____
_____
_____
_____
_____
_____
_____
_____
_____
_____
_____

NOTES

November _____

Due Date	Bill Description	Amount Due	Amount Paid	Paid Date	Confirmation Number	Notes

Notes for the Month

_____
_____
_____
_____
_____
_____
_____
_____
_____
_____
_____

December _____

Due Date	Bill Description	Amount Due	Amount Paid	Paid Date	Confirmation Number	Notes

Notes for the Month

_____
_____
_____
_____
_____
_____
_____
_____
_____
_____

NOTES

JANUARY _____

Due Date	Bill Description	Amount Due	Amount Paid	Paid Date	Confirmation Number	Notes

Notes for the Month

_____
_____
_____
_____
_____
_____
_____
_____
_____
_____

NOTES

February _____

Due Date	Bill Description	Amount Due	Amount Paid	Paid Date	Confirmation Number	Notes

Notes for the Month

_____
_____
_____
_____
_____
_____
_____
_____
_____
_____
_____

NOTES

March _____

Due Date	Bill Description	Amount Due	Amount Paid	Paid Date	Confirmation Number	Notes

Notes for the Month

NOTES

April _____

Due Date	Bill Description	Amount Due	Amount Paid	Paid Date	Confirmation Number	Notes

Notes for the Month

_____
_____
_____
_____
_____
_____
_____
_____
_____
_____
_____
_____

NOTES

May _____

Due Date	Bill Description	Amount Due	Amount Paid	Paid Date	Confirmation Number	Notes

Notes for the Month

_____
_____
_____
_____
_____
_____
_____
_____
_____
_____
_____
_____

NOTES

June _____

Due Date	Bill Description	Amount Due	Amount Paid	Paid Date	Confirmation Number	Notes

Notes for the Month

_____

_____

_____

_____

_____

_____

_____

_____

_____

_____

_____

NOTES

July _____

Due Date	Bill Description	Amount Due	Amount Paid	Paid Date	Confirmation Number	Notes

Notes for the Month

_____
_____
_____
_____
_____
_____
_____
_____
_____
_____

NOTES

August _____

Due Date	Bill Description	Amount Due	Amount Paid	Paid Date	Confirmation Number	Notes

Notes for the Month

_____

_____

_____

_____

_____

_____

_____

_____

_____

_____

_____

_____

September _____

Due Date	Bill Description	Amount Due	Amount Paid	Paid Date	Confirmation Number	Notes

Notes for the Month

_____
_____
_____
_____
_____
_____
_____
_____
_____
_____

NOTES

October _____

Due Date	Bill Description	Amount Due	Amount Paid	Paid Date	Confirmation Number	Notes

Notes for the Month

_____
_____
_____
_____
_____
_____
_____
_____
_____
_____
_____

November _____

Due Date	Bill Description	Amount Due	Amount Paid	Paid Date	Confirmation Number	Notes

Notes for the Month

NOTES

December _____

Due Date	Bill Description	Amount Due	Amount Paid	Paid Date	Confirmation Number	Notes

Notes for the Month

_____
_____
_____
_____
_____
_____
_____
_____
_____
_____

NOTES

JANUARY _____

Due Date	Bill Description	Amount Due	Amount Paid	Paid Date	Confirmation Number	Notes

Notes for the Month

_____
_____
_____
_____
_____
_____
_____
_____
_____
_____
_____

NOTES

February _____

Due Date	Bill Description	Amount Due	Amount Paid	Paid Date	Confirmation Number	Notes

Notes for the Month

_____
_____
_____
_____
_____
_____
_____
_____
_____
_____
_____

NOTES

March _____

Due Date	Bill Description	Amount Due	Amount Paid	Paid Date	Confirmation Number	Notes

Notes for the Month

NOTES

April _____

Due Date	Bill Description	Amount Due	Amount Paid	Paid Date	Confirmation Number	Notes

Notes for the Month

_____
_____
_____
_____
_____
_____
_____
_____
_____
_____
_____

NOTES

May _____

Due Date	Bill Description	Amount Due	Amount Paid	Paid Date	Confirmation Number	Notes

Notes for the Month

_____
_____
_____
_____
_____
_____
_____
_____
_____
_____
_____

NOTES

June _____

Due Date	Bill Description	Amount Due	Amount Paid	Paid Date	Confirmation Number	Notes

Notes for the Month

_____
_____
_____
_____
_____
_____
_____
_____
_____
_____
_____

NOTES

July _____

Due Date	Bill Description	Amount Due	Amount Paid	Paid Date	Confirmation Number	Notes

Notes for the Month

_____
_____
_____
_____
_____
_____
_____
_____
_____
_____
_____
_____

NOTES

August _____

Due Date	Bill Description	Amount Due	Amount Paid	Paid Date	Confirmation Number	Notes

Notes for the Month

_____
_____
_____
_____
_____
_____
_____
_____
_____
_____
_____
_____

NOTES

September _____

Due Date	Bill Description	Amount Due	Amount Paid	Paid Date	Confirmation Number	Notes

Notes for the Month

_____
_____
_____
_____
_____
_____
_____
_____
_____
_____
_____
_____

NOTES

October _____

Due Date	Bill Description	Amount Due	Amount Paid	Paid Date	Confirmation Number	Notes

Notes for the Month

_____
_____
_____
_____
_____
_____
_____
_____
_____
_____
_____
_____

NOTES

November _____

Due Date	Bill Description	Amount Due	Amount Paid	Paid Date	Confirmation Number	Notes

Notes for the Month

_____
_____
_____
_____
_____
_____
_____
_____
_____
_____
_____

NOTES

December _____

Due Date	Bill Description	Amount Due	Amount Paid	Paid Date	Confirmation Number	Notes

Notes for the Month

_____
_____
_____
_____
_____
_____
_____
_____
_____
_____
_____

NOTES

JANUARY _____

Due Date	Bill Description	Amount Due	Amount Paid	Paid Date	Confirmation Number	Notes

Notes for the Month

_____
_____
_____
_____
_____
_____
_____
_____
_____
_____

NOTES

February _____

Due Date	Bill Description	Amount Due	Amount Paid	Paid Date	Confirmation Number	Notes

Notes for the Month

_____

_____

_____

_____

_____

_____

_____

_____

_____

_____

_____

March _____

Due Date	Bill Description	Amount Due	Amount Paid	Paid Date	Confirmation Number	Notes

Notes for the Month

_____
_____
_____
_____
_____
_____
_____
_____
_____
_____

NOTES

April _____

Due Date	Bill Description	Amount Due	Amount Paid	Paid Date	Confirmation Number	Notes

Notes for the Month

NOTES

May _____

Due Date	Bill Description	Amount Due	Amount Paid	Paid Date	Confirmation Number	Notes

Notes for the Month

NOTES

June _____

Due Date	Bill Description	Amount Due	Amount Paid	Paid Date	Confirmation Number	Notes

Notes for the Month

_____

_____

_____

_____

_____

_____

_____

_____

_____

_____

_____

July _____

Due Date	Bill Description	Amount Due	Amount Paid	Paid Date	Confirmation Number	Notes

Notes for the Month

NOTES

August _____

Due Date	Bill Description	Amount Due	Amount Paid	Paid Date	Confirmation Number	Notes

Notes for the Month

_____
_____
_____
_____
_____
_____
_____
_____
_____
_____
_____

September _____

Due Date	Bill Description	Amount Due	Amount Paid	Paid Date	Confirmation Number	Notes

Notes for the Month

_____
_____
_____
_____
_____
_____
_____
_____
_____
_____
_____

October _____

Due Date	Bill Description	Amount Due	Amount Paid	Paid Date	Confirmation Number	Notes

Notes for the Month

_____
_____
_____
_____
_____
_____
_____
_____
_____
_____
_____

NOTES

November _____

Due Date	Bill Description	Amount Due	Amount Paid	Paid Date	Confirmation Number	Notes

Notes for the Month

_____
_____
_____
_____
_____
_____
_____
_____
_____
_____
_____

NOTES

December _____

Due Date	Bill Description	Amount Due	Amount Paid	Paid Date	Confirmation Number	Notes

Notes for the Month

NOTES

JANUARY _____

Due Date	Bill Description	Amount Due	Amount Paid	Paid Date	Confirmation Number	Notes

Notes for the Month

_____
_____
_____
_____
_____
_____
_____
_____
_____
_____

NOTES

February _____

Due Date	Bill Description	Amount Due	Amount Paid	Paid Date	Confirmation Number	Notes

Notes for the Month

_____

_____

_____

_____

_____

_____

_____

_____

_____

_____

March _____

Due Date	Bill Description	Amount Due	Amount Paid	Paid Date	Confirmation Number	Notes

Notes for the Month

_____
_____
_____
_____
_____
_____
_____
_____
_____
_____
_____

NOTES

April _____

Due Date	Bill Description	Amount Due	Amount Paid	Paid Date	Confirmation Number	Notes

Notes for the Month

_____
_____
_____
_____
_____
_____
_____
_____
_____
_____
_____

NOTES

May _____

Due Date	Bill Description	Amount Due	Amount Paid	Paid Date	Confirmation Number	Notes

Notes for the Month

_____
_____
_____
_____
_____
_____
_____
_____
_____
_____
_____

NOTES

June _____

Due Date	Bill Description	Amount Due	Amount Paid	Paid Date	Confirmation Number	Notes

Notes for the Month

_____

_____

_____

_____

_____

_____

_____

_____

_____

_____

_____

July _____

Due Date	Bill Description	Amount Due	Amount Paid	Paid Date	Confirmation Number	Notes

Notes for the Month

_____
_____
_____
_____
_____
_____
_____
_____
_____
_____
_____

NOTES

August _____

Due Date	Bill Description	Amount Due	Amount Paid	Paid Date	Confirmation Number	Notes

Notes for the Month

_____
_____
_____
_____
_____
_____
_____
_____
_____
_____

NOTES

September _____

Due Date	Bill Description	Amount Due	Amount Paid	Paid Date	Confirmation Number	Notes

Notes for the Month

_____
_____
_____
_____
_____
_____
_____
_____
_____
_____
_____

NOTES

October _____

Due Date	Bill Description	Amount Due	Amount Paid	Paid Date	Confirmation Number	Notes

Notes for the Month

_____
_____
_____
_____
_____
_____
_____
_____
_____
_____
_____

NOTES

November _____

Due Date	Bill Description	Amount Due	Amount Paid	Paid Date	Confirmation Number	Notes

Notes for the Month

_____
_____
_____
_____
_____
_____
_____
_____
_____
_____
_____

NOTES

December _____

Due Date	Bill Description	Amount Due	Amount Paid	Paid Date	Confirmation Number	Notes

Notes for the Month

_____
_____
_____
_____
_____
_____
_____
_____
_____
_____
_____

NOTES

NOTES

NOTES

www.ingramcontent.com/pod-product-compliance
Lightning Source LLC
Chambersburg PA
CBHW081600220526
45468CB00010B/2712